A Guide for Using

Freckle Juice, The Pain and the Great One, and The One in the Middle Is the Green Kangaroo

in the Classroom

Based on the books written by Judy Blume

*This guide was written by **Julia Johnson***
*and illustrated by **Bruce Hedges***

Teacher Created Materials, Inc.
6421 Industry Way
Westminster, CA 92683
www.teachercreated.com
©1998 Teacher Created Materials
Reprinted, 2000
Made in U.S.A.
ISBN 1-57690-345-1

Table of Contents

 ◆ Quiz
 ◆ Hands-On Project—*Point of View*
 ◆ Cooperative Learning Activity—*Baseball Roles*
 ◆ Curriculum Connection—Language Arts: *Dear Judy . . .*
 ◆ Into Your Life—*Now I Can Do It!*

 ◆ Quiz
 ◆ Hands-On Project—*In the Middle*
 ◆ Cooperative Learning Activity—*Practice Makes Perfect*
 ◆ Curriculum Connection—Science: *Jumping Experiment*
 ◆ Into Your Life—*My Family*

 ◆ Quiz
 ◆ Hands-On Project—*Kangaroo Research*
 ◆ Cooperative Learning Activity—*Let's Play!*
 ◆ Curriculum Connection—Language Arts: *Green Kangaroo Word Search*
 ◆ Into Your Life—*A Star Is Born*

 ◆ Quiz
 ◆ Hands-On Project—*Fact or Opinion?*
 ◆ Cooperative Learning Activity—*I Like Your . . .*
 ◆ Curriculum Connection—Math: *Allowance*
 ◆ Into Your Life—*Daydreaming*

 ◆ Quiz
 ◆ Hands-On Project—*No-Cook Recipe Fun*
 ◆ Cooperative Learning Activity—*Make a Recipe*
 ◆ Curriculum Connection—Science: *Chemistry Experiments*
 ◆ Into Your Life—*I Like My . . . .*

 Book Report Ideas
 Crossword Puzzle

Introduction

A good book can touch our lives like a good friend. Within its pages are words and characters that can inspire us to achieve our highest ideals. We can turn to it for companionship, recreation, comfort, knowledge, and guidance. It can make us laugh out aloud or cry at its tenderness. It can also give us a cherished story to hold in our hearts forever.

In Literature Units, great care has been taken to select books that are sure to become good friends!

Teachers who use this literature unit will discover the following features to supplement their own valuable ideas.

- Sample Lesson Plans

- Pre-reading Activities

- A Biographical Sketch of the Author

- Book Summaries

- Vocabulary Lists and Suggested Vocabulary Ideas

- Chapters grouped for study with each section including the following:

    -*a quiz*

    -*a hands-on project*

    -*a cooperative learning activity*

    -*cross curricular connections*

    -*an extension into the reader's life*

- Post-reading Activities

- Book Report Ideas

- A Culminating Activity

- Three Options for Unit Tests

- A Bibliography

- An Answer Key

We are confident that this unit will be a valuable addition to your planning, and we hope that as you use our ideas, your students will increase the circle of friends they have in books!

Sample Lesson Plan

Each of the lessons suggested below can take from one to several days to complete.

LESSON 1
- Introduce and complete some or all of the pre-reading activities. (page 5)
- Read About the Author with your students. (page 6)
- Introduce the vocabulary for Section 1. (page 10)

LESSON 2
- Read *The Pain and the Great One*. As you read, place the vocabulary words in the context of the story and discuss their meanings.
- Choose a vocabulary activity. (page 11)
- Practice identifying point of view. (page 13)
- Explore point of view using baseball. (page 14)
- Write a letter to Judy Blume. (page 15)
- List skills acquired since first grade. (page 16)
- Administer the Section 1 quiz. (page 12)
- Introduce some or all of the pre-reading activities. (page 5)
- Introduce the vocabulary for Section 2. (page 10)

LESSON 3
- Read the first half of *The One in the Middle Is the Green Kangaroo*. Place the vocabulary words in context and discuss their meanings.
- Choose a vocabulary activity. (page 11)
- See different meanings of *middle*. (page 18)
- Practice tongue twisters. (page 19)
- Conduct a jumping experiment. (page 20)
- Write about family. (page 22)
- Administer the Section 2 quiz. (page 17)
- Introduce the vocabulary for Section 3. (page 10)

LESSON 4
- Read the second half of *The One in the Middle Is the Green Kangaroo*. Place the vocabulary words in context and discuss their meanings.
- Choose a vocabulary activity. (page 11)
- Research real-life kangaroos. (page 24)
- Rehearse a scene from a play. (page 25)
- Complete a word search puzzle. (page 26)
- Write about being a star. (page 27)
- Administer the Section 3 quiz. (page 23)
- Introduce some or all of the pre-reading activities on page 5.
- Introduce the vocabulary for Section 4. (page 10)

LESSON 5
- Read chapters 1 and 2 of *Freckle Juice*. Place the vocabulary words in context and discuss their meanings.
- Choose a vocabulary activity. (page 11)
- Identify facts and opinions. (page 29)
- Tell what you like about others. (page 30)
- Practice spending an allowance. (page 31)
- Describe a daydream. (page 32)
- Administer the Section 4 quiz. (page 28)
- Introduce the vocabulary for Section 5. (page 10)

LESSON 6
- Read chapters 3 through 5 of *Freckle Juice*. Place the vocabulary words in context and discuss their meanings.
- Choose a vocabulary activity. (page 11)
- Make no-cook recipes. (page 34)
- Write a recipe. (page 35)
- Conduct a chemistry experiment. (page 36)
- Write what you like about yourself. (page 37)
- Administer the Section 5 quiz. (page 33)

LESSON 7
- Discuss any questions your students may have about the stories.
- Assign book reports. (page 38)
- Complete the crossword puzzle. (page 39)
- Begin work on the culminating activity. (pages 40–42)

LESSON 8
- Administer unit tests 1, 2, and/or 3. (pages 43–45)
- Discuss the test answers and responses.
- Discuss the students' opinions and enjoyment of the books.
- Complete the culminating activity.

Before the Book

Before you begin reading each of the three Judy Blume books with your students, do some pre-reading activities to stimulate interest and enhance comprehension. Here are some activities that might work well in your class.

Before Any of the Books

1. Predict what the story might be about just by hearing the title.
2. Predict what the story might be about just by looking at the cover illustration.
3. Discuss families with different numbers of children and relate the books to the types of families they present:
   - *The Pain and the Great One*—two children
   - *The One in the Middle Is the Green Kangaroo*—three children
   - *Freckle Juice*—only child
4. Have each student tell how many children are in his or her family. Collect and summarize the information in a class graph.
5. Discuss other books by Judy Blume that students may have read or heard about.

Before *The Pain and the Great One*

1. Answer these questions:
   Are you interested in stories . . .
   - about families?
   - about brothers and sisters?
   - about how things look through other people's eyes?
2. Answer these questions:
   Would you ever . . .
   - complain about your brother or sister?
   - be jealous of your brother or sister?

Before *The One in the Middle Is the Green Kangaroo*

1. Answer these questions:
   Are you interested in stories . . .
   - about families?
   - about performing a play?
2. Answer these questions:
   Would you ever . . .
   - be in a play?
   - speak in front of people on a stage?

Before *Freckle Juice*

1. Answer these questions:
   Are you interested in stories . . .
   - about wanting to look different?
   - about secret recipes?
2. Answer these questions:
   Would you ever . . .
   - do something silly in school?
   - spend your allowance foolishly?
   - want to be like someone else?

About the Author

Judy Blume was born in Elizabeth, New Jersey, in 1938. Her father was a dentist. Her family liked to read. "My mother was shy and quiet and very well organized. She loved to read. When I came home from school in the afternoon she was always there waiting, curled up in her favorite chair, reading a book." Judy liked movies, radio shows, and books and started dance lessons at age three. She liked going to the library. Her favorite book was *Madeline* by Ludwig Bemelmans. She loved it so much that she hid it so her mother wouldn't be able to return it to the library.

In school, Judy liked English but did not like science. She worked on the school paper, sang in the chorus, and studied dance. She went to school at NYU and got her degree in early childhood education. Judy got married in 1959 and had two children: Randy Lee, who is now an airline pilot, and Lawrence Andrew, who is now a film maker.

Judy began writing in 1966 when her children were three and five. She had studied to be a teacher but decided to write children's books instead. "I read my kids a lot of books, and I guess I just decided— Well, I could do that too." She started with books for young children, similar to those from Dr. Seuss. She tried for two years to get her books published. They were rejected by many publishers. In one week she received six letters from publishers rejecting her books. But she didn't give up. Instead, she changed the type of book she was writing. ". . . it occurred to me that what I really loved most was to read novels. I thought it would be fun to write books for young people—the kind of books I'd wished I'd had to read when I was young. Books about real life."

In 1969 Judy's first book was finally published. It was called *The One in the Middle Is the Green Kangaroo.* She continues to write honest novels based on her own memories of childhood and adolescence. Her readers have written her thousands of letters saying that they love her books and that they are just like their own lives. Her books for children include *Iggie's House; Are You There, God? It's Me, Margaret; Then Again, Maybe I Won't; Tales of a Fourth Grade Nothing; It's Not the End of the World; Otherwise Known as Sheila the Great; Blubber; Starring Sally J. Freedman as Herself; Superfudge;* and *Tiger Eyes.*

You can write to Judy Blume at this address:

> Judy Blume
> c/o Harold Ober Associates, Inc.
> 425 Madison Ave.
> New York, NY 10017
> e-mail: JUDY@JUDYBLUME.COM

The Pain and the Great One

by Judy Blume, illustrated by Irene Trivas

Dell Publishing, 1974

Summary

The first half of this two-part book is told from the point of view of an older sister. The Pain is a younger brother, in first grade, who acts like a baby and gets treated like one. His older sister thinks he is spoiled, gets special privileges, and makes a mess of the house. He can't get to breakfast on time or dress himself for school. Mom makes a big deal over his first grade schoolwork. He gets dessert even if he doesn't eat all his dinner. He doesn't even know how to take a bath without making a mess. One night, big sister's request to stay up later than The Pain is granted, and she discovers it's not so much fun to be able to stay up without him. But he is still a pain. He interrupts her phone calls and wrecks her cities made of blocks. And the cat sleeps on his bed, even though big sister feeds her. Worst of all, Mom and Daddy love him more than her.

The second half of the book is told from the point of view of a younger brother. The Great One is an older sister, in third grade, who has convinced Mom and Daddy that she's smart because she's older. Her younger brother believes she thinks she's great just because she can do things he can't. She plays the piano, and you can tell the songs are real. She gets to feed the cat just because she knows how to work the can opener. So of course the cat likes her better. She is allowed to hold their aunt's baby, even though the baby sleeps and gets changed in his room. She gets to call her friends on the phone. She invites her friends over and builds cities of blocks with them. One day, little brother's request to play with the blocks by himself is granted, and he discovers it's not so much fun to play alone. But he still thinks she is great. She can even swim, while he is afraid to put his face in the water. Worst of all, Mom and Daddy love her more than him.

The One in the Middle Is the Green Kangaroo

by Judy Blume, illustrated by Amy Aitken
Bradbury Press, 1981

Summary

Freddy Dissel is a middle child with an older brother, Mike, and a baby sister, Ellen. Freddy gets Mike's hand-me-downs and has to give up his room to Ellen. He is too young to play with Mike's friends, and Ellen is too young to play his games. He feels like a "great big middle nothing."

Freddy hears about a school play and decides it is his chance to do something special. He tells his teacher, Ms. Gumber, he wants to be in the play. She says the play is only for fifth and sixth graders. Seeing Freddy's disappointment, she offers to talk to Ms. Matson, the teacher in charge of the play, to see if there are any parts for second graders. Ms. Gumber gets Freddy a chance to try out for a special part in the play. He goes to the auditorium and goes on stage for the first time. Ms. Matson has him jump and talk very loudly. She gives him the part of the Green Kangaroo. At dinner that night, Freddy's brother and sister are a little jealous of his getting the part, but his parents are proud.

Freddy practices hard for his part, both at school and at home. He jumps like a Green Kangaroo and even dreams of Green Kangaroos. Finally, the day of the play comes. His entire family and some neighbors will be there. After lunch, his teacher tells him it is time to go and wishes him luck. He puts on his costume and waits backstage with the older students. He is nervous. At last, it is time for him to go onstage in front of the audience. He does his job and starts the play as the Green Kangaroo. In spite of being nervous, he does a perfect job. The audience likes him and the funny play, and the teacher in charge of the play gives him a special curtain call.

After the play, Freddy does not mind being the middle child any more. He feels good just being himself.

Freckle Juice

by Judy Blume, illustrated by Sonia O. Lisker
Four Winds Press, 1971

Summary

Daydreaming in class, Andrew wishes he had freckles like Nicky, who sits in front of him at school. Sharon, who is always making faces at Andrew, offers to sell him her family's "secret recipe" for freckle juice. It will cost him 50 cents, which is five weeks allowance for Andrew.

Andrew decides to buy the recipe and brings five dimes to school to give Sharon. In the middle of the sale of the recipe, Andrew is caught by his teacher, Miss Kelly, who takes away the recipe he has already paid for. Fortunately, she gives it back to him after school.

Andrew's mother is at a neighbor's house, playing cards for the afternoon. Andrew goes home and makes freckle juice while his mother is next door playing cards. The recipe includes a strange mixture of ingredients, including onion, vinegar, mayonnaise, and grape juice. It is a terrible concoction, but Andrew drinks it anyway. It makes Andrew sick to his stomach, and his mother is alarmed to find him lying on the floor when she gets home. He misses his dinner and the next day at school.

Rather than returning to class with no freckles, Andrew uses a blue Magic Marker to draw freckles on his face. The class laughs at his blue freckles, but he sits in class all day with his blue freckles. At the end of the day, Miss Kelly gives him her secret formula freckle remover to wash them away. She also tells him she thinks he is handsome without freckles. Nicky reveals that he hates his freckles, and Sharon offers to sell him her family's "secret recipe" for freckle remover.

Vocabulary Lists

Section 1

buildings	disgusting	enough	piano	remember
dessert	drawer	ordinary	reason	thought

Section 2

auditorium	important	middle	sandwich	special
either	kangaroo	proud	scream	squeezed

Section 3

audience	bow	costume	neighbors	stage
backstage	clapped	laugh	practice	stomach

Section 4

allowance	combination	freckles	inspect	recipe
attention	figure	giggle	olive	tongue

Section 5

absolutely	cabinet	handsome	ingredients	quart
ambulance	formula	hospital	reflection	whisper

Vocabulary Activity Ideas

You can help your students to learn and retain the vocabulary in the three books by providing them with interesting vocabulary activities. Here are a few ideas to try.

◆ Challenge your students to a **vocabulary bee**. This is similar to a spelling bee, but in addition to spelling the word correctly, the game participants must also correctly define each word.

◆ Ask your students to make their own **crossword** or **word search puzzles**, using the vocabulary words from the books.

◆ Play **20 clues** with the entire class. In this game, one student selects a vocabulary word and gives clues about the word, one by one, until someone in the class can guess and spell the word.

◆ Play **vocabulary charades**. In this game, vocabulary words are acted out by one student while others guess the word.

◆ Play **vocabulary concentration**. The goal of this game is to match vocabulary words with their definitions. Divide the class into groups of two to five students. Have the students make two sets of cards the same size and color. On one set, have them write the vocabulary words. On the second set, have them write the definitions. All cards are mixed together and placed facedown on a table. A player picks two cards. If the pair matches the word with its definition, the player keeps the cards and takes another turn. If the cards do not match, they are returned to their places facedown, and another player takes a turn. Players must concentrate to remember the locations of words and definitions. The game continues until all matches have been made. The winner is the player with the most cards at the end of the game.

◆ Have the students work together to create an **illustrated dictionary** of vocabulary words.

◆ Ask your students to write a **sentence** or **paragraph** that includes as many vocabulary words as possible.

◆ Encourage students to keep a **vocabulary journal** where they can write words they are not familiar with and which did not appear on the vocabulary list.

◆ Challenge the students to find **synonyms** or **antonyms** for the vocabulary words.

◆ Have the students use these words as their weekly **spelling list**.

You probably have many more ideas to add to this list. Try them! Practicing selected words through these types of activities increases student interest in, and retention of, vocabulary.

Quiz

1. On the back of this paper, write a one-paragraph summary of the major events in *The Pain and the Great One*.

2. Who is The Pain? _____

   _____

3. Who is The Great One? _____

   _____

4. Name three things The Pain does that bother his sister.

   _____

   _____

   _____

5. Name three things The Great One does better than her brother.

   _____

   _____

   _____

6. Who gets to feed the cat? _____

7. Why wasn't it fun to stay up late without The Pain? _____

   _____

8. Why do you think The Pain does things to make his sister mad?_____

   _____

   _____

   _____

9. What would you do if you were The Pain's brother or sister? _____

   _____

   _____

   _____

10. Who do you think Mom and Dad love best? Why?_____

    _____

    _____

Point of View

The Pain and the Great One is one story written from two different points of view. The first half is written from the older sister's point of view. The second half is written from the younger brother's point of view. Things can look very different, depending on your point of view!

Let's see if you can identify a point of view. Pretend that each of the following statements was made by one of the characters in the book. Circle the character you think said each statement.

1. *I'm lucky because I have two children to pet me.*	Pain	Mom	Cat
2. *The cat doesn't like me because I don't feed it.*	Pain	Dad	Great One
3. *I think the Great One is smart and pretty.*	Pain	Mom	Great One
4. *The Great One thinks she's better than me.*	Cat	Pain	Dad
5. *The Pain acts like a baby.*	Mom	Great One	Pain
6. *Every child is special and loved.*	Great One	Pain	Mom or Dad
7. *I wish I didn't have a little brother.*	Dad	Pain	Great One
8. *I love both of our children very much.*	Pain	Cat	Mom
9. *I wish I got to do special things because I was older.*	Pain	Great One	Dad
10. *It's no fun being the youngest.*	Great One	Pain	Dad
11. *Older children should get to do more things.*	Mom	Great One	Pain

Make up a statement you think shows each of these character's point of view:

Pain_____

_____

Great One _____

_____

Mom or Dad _____

_____

Baseball Roles

This activity allows students to assume different points of view in a baseball game.

Divide the class into groups of four students. Explain that they are going to do an activity related to baseball.

Show a video clip of a home run being hit. (See bibliography for movie suggestions.) Use appropriate scenes only. Parents' permission and principal's authorization will be needed for showing commercial fims.

Now, give each group a set of four cards. On each card, a different point of view has been written, including "the hitter," "the fielder," "the ball," and "the bat." Have each group member choose one card, but ask them not to show one another their cards. Write the four points of view on the board and discuss them to make sure everyone understands their meanings.

Hitter

Now show the video clip again, asking each student to pay attention to the home run from his or her assigned point of view.

In groups, have each student describe the events, feelings, and results of the home run hit from his or her assigned point of view.

If time permits, have the students reshuffle the cards and choose a new point of view to describe.

Fielder

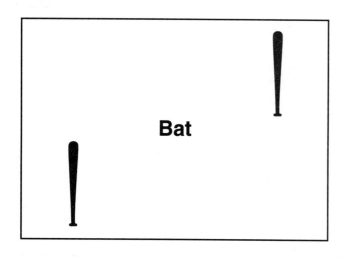

Bat

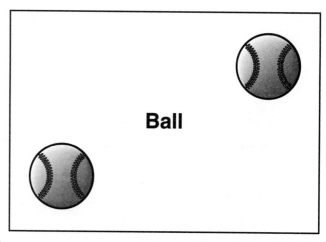

Ball

Dear Judy . . .

Many children write letters to Judy Blume after they read her books. She has even published a book of some of the letters she has received. Your teacher has an address to which you can send a letter to Judy Blume. Write her a letter telling her about your feelings after reading *The Pain and the Great One*.

On a separate sheet of paper, write your letter to Judy Blume. Use the following letter-writing format or one your teacher gives you.

Here are some things you could write about:

- Did you like the book? Why or why not?

- Did anyone in the book remind you of someone in your family? Who? How?

- Did you like the way the book used different points of view? Did one of the points of view sound like you?

- Do you have a brother or sister? How do you get along with him or her?

- Did you learn anything from the book?

- How did reading the book make you feel?

- Would you like to read other books by Judy Blume?

Date

Dear Judy Blume,
(Skip a line.)

Body of Letter
(Indent the first paragraph.)
(Indent the beginning of each paragraph.)

(skip a line before closing)
Sincerely,

Your signature

Now I Can Do It!

The Pain is a first grader. The Great One is in third grade. The Great One can do many things The Pain cannot. She can swim, play the piano, hold a baby, dial the telephone, and build cities with blocks. These are all things The Pain will be able to do when he gets older.

Name 10 things you can do now that you could not do when you were in first grade.

1. _____

   _____

2. _____

   _____

3. _____

   _____

4. _____

   _____

5. _____

   _____

6. _____

   _____

7. _____

   _____

8. _____

   _____

9. _____

   _____

10. _____

   _____

Quiz

1. On the back of this paper, write a one-paragraph summary of the major events in the first half of *The One in the Middle Is the Green Kangaroo.*

2. Freddy has a(n)_____brother and a(n)_____sister.

3. Why do you think Freddy wanted to be in the play? _____

    _____

    _____

4. Where did Freddy have to go to show Ms. Matson what he could do in the play?

    _____

5. What did Freddy have to do to show Ms. Matson what he could do in the play?

    _____

6. The rest of the kids in the play are_____th and_____th graders.

7. What did Mike do when he found out Freddy was going to be in a play?

    _____

    _____

8. What do you think Freddy's mom thought about Freddy being in the play?

    _____

    _____

    _____

9. What do you think Freddy's brother Mike thought about Freddy being in the play?

    _____

    _____

    _____

10. How do you think you would feel if you were a middle child? _____

    _____

    _____

    _____

In the Middle

Freddy is the middle child in his family. He has one older brother and one younger sister. Here are some "middle" puzzles for you to solve.

Circle the middle child in each family:

1.	Joe, 3 years old	Mary, 5 years old	Matt, 4 years old
2.	Shawna, 9 years old	Jerome, 4 years old	Tasha, 6 years old
3.	Jose, 2 years old	Maria, 4 years old	Esteban, 6 months old
4.	Anna, 12 years old	Erica, 14 years old	Tuan, 10 years old
5.	Amy, 5 years old	Scott, 7 years old	Daniel, 6 years old

Find the middle of each ruler and put an arrow there.

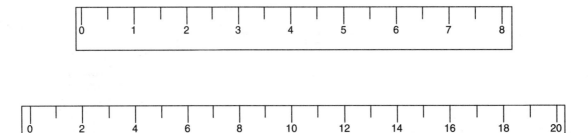

Cut out the things you like on your hamburger. Put together your hamburger with the meat in the middle.

| Top Bun | Bottom Bun | Meat | Ketchup |
| Cheese | Lettuce | Mustard | Pickle |

Practice Makes Perfect

Freddy spends a lot of time practicing for his part as the kangaroo in the school play. Practice makes difficult tasks easier. See how practice can help you improve.

With a partner, take turns reading one of the following tongue twisters. Pretty hard? Now, practice the same tongue twister, saying it very slowly. Practice saying it six more times. Have your partner keep count for you. Finally, say the tongue twister one more time. It should have become easier to say since the first time!

She sells sea shells by the seashore.

Peter Piper picked a peck of pickled
peppers.

How much wood would a woodchuck
chuck,
If a woodchuck could chuck wood?

A big black bug bit
a big black bear,
making the big black bear
bleed blood.

Big Billy, who had a big belly, was also a
big bully.

Mrs. Smith's Fish Sauce Shop

I can think of thin things, six thin things;
can you?

Hard-hearted Harold hit Henry hard
with a hickory-handled hammer.
Henry howled horribly and hurriedly
hobbled home.

Rubber Baby Buggy Bumpers

This is a zither.

If you and your partner have time, try another tongue twister or keep practicing to say yours in front of the class.

Jumping Experiment

Freddy did a lot of jumping as the Green Kangaroo. You can do a scientific experiment about jumping and report your conclusions to the rest of the class. You'll need a partner to work with, a measuring tape, the blank form on the next page, and a pencil.

1. Talk with your partner and come up with two ideas that you think will make you jump farther. Write those in the *Purpose* section.

2. A hypothesis is a prediction of what you think will happen. Talk with your partner about what you think will happen when you try your jumping ideas. Write what you think will happen in the *Hypothesis* section.

3. Write what you will do during your experiment in the *Procedure* section. Do not do the experiment yet. Just write what you're going to do. Here is a suggestion:

   - Jump normally.
   - Measure how far you jumped.
   - Try the first idea for making you jump farther.
   - Measure how far you jumped.
   - Try the second idea for making you jump farther.
   - Measure how far you jumped.

4. Now, do your experiment. Have your partner help you measure. Record your results and your partner's results in the *Results* section.

5. Study the results of your experiment. Did your ideas make you jump farther? Was your hypothesis correct? Write your conclusions about your experiment in the *Conclusions* section.

Jumping Experiment *(cont.)*

Purpose

To find out if the following ideas will make me jump farther:

Idea 1 _____

Idea 2 _____

Hypothesis

I predict that . . .

_____

_____

_____

_____

_____

Procedure

_____

_____

_____

_____

_____

_____

Results

	Normal Jump	Idea #1 Jump	Idea #2 Jump
You			
Your Partner			

Conclusions

_____

_____

_____

_____

_____

My Family

There are many different types of families. Freddy's family has three children, a mother, and a father. The children are two boys and one girl. Other families may have fewer or more children, parents, grandparents, or others.

Write a composition about your family. Here are some suggestions to get you started.

In the first paragraph, describe your family. You may want to include answers to these questions or write other things you think of.

- Are you an only child, the oldest, the youngest, the middle child, or somewhere in between?

- Are the children in your family all boys, all girls, or both?

- Who are the adults that live with you—mother, father, grandmother, uncle, someone else?

- Are there other family members whom you see often, like aunts, cousins, or grandparents?

In the second paragraph, describe the good things about being part of your family.

- What do you like best about your family?

- Is there something a person in your family does that makes you happy? What is it? Why does it make you happy? Include as many things as you want.

- We don't always like everything we need to do in a family. Freddy didn't like wearing his brother's hand-me-down clothes. Describe something your family does for the good of everyone.

In the third paragraph, describe your family traditions.

- Is there something that your family does together every day or every week? Do you eat dinner together, rent videos a certain night of the week, play certain games, or attend a religious service together?

- Describe something you do often with all or part of your family.

Quiz

1. On the back of this paper, write a one-paragraph summary of the major events in the second half of *The One in the Middle Is the Green Kangaroo.*

2. What did Freddy do to practice for the play? _____

_____

_____

3. Who came to see Freddy in the play? _____

_____

4. What does "break a leg" mean?_____

5. Describe Freddy's costume._____

_____

_____

6. Why do you think Freddy's stomach "bounced up and down" before the play started?

_____

_____

7. How would you feel if you were all alone on a stage in front of an audience?

_____

_____

_____

8. What did Freddy have to do to pretend to be the Green Kangaroo?_____

_____

_____

9. Did the audience like the play? How do you know? _____

_____

_____

10. Why did Freddy feel so great after he was in the play? _____

_____

_____

_____

Kangaroo Research

Learn more about real kangaroos by finding the answers to the following questions in your classroom, in the library, or on the Internet.   Write a paragraph about kangaroos, using the information you find. Here are some questions to get you started.

- Where do kangaroos live?
- How far can a kangaroo jump?
- What is a baby kangaroo called?
- Where does a baby kangaroo live? For how long?
- What do kangaroos eat?
- Why do kangaroos have long tails?
- How many types of kangaroos are there?
- What is a *wallaby*?
- What is a *marsupial*?

If you have extra time when you finish your work, draw a picture of a kangaroo, using a picture you find to help you.

My Kangaroo Paragraph

Let's Play!

Freddy got to be the kangaroo in a play at school. Plays are special kinds of stories, and they are written in a special way. Plays have scenes instead of chapters. Characters take turns reading lines instead of paragraphs. Plays include directions for characters to move and act.

Television shows and movies are plays put on film or videotape. This is your chance to be part of one scene in a play. Your teacher will assign you to a group and tell you which character you will be. Read the scene to yourself once. Then find your lines and read them again to yourself. When you are finished, let your group know. Now you are ready to rehearse the scene. Whoever is the JUDGE should start the scene by reading the first line. Take turns reading the lines in order. Now stand up and add actions that make sense with the lines. You're an actor!

Scene: The Tortoise and the Hare Get Ready to Race

JUDGE: Are you ready to hear the rules for the race?

TORTOISE: Yes.

HARE: Yes.

FAN: Let's go. Let's start this race!

JUDGE: Here are the rules: No pushing or tripping. No short cuts. No cheating. Mr. Tortoise, do you agree to follow the rules?

TORTOISE: Yes, Judge.

JUDGE: Mr. Hare, do you agree to follow the rules?

HARE: Yes, yes. Let's go.

FAN: Come on, come on. I don't have all day to wait for this race to start!

JUDGE: OK, I want you to shake hands.

(Tortoise and Hare shake hands.)

TORTOISE: Good luck to you, Mr. Hare.

HARE: Ha ha! I don't need any luck. I'm going be finished before you even start!

TORTOISE: I'm glad you are confident, Mr. Hare. We shall see who wins in the end.

FAN: Please start the race. I'm getting hungry.

JUDGE: Now, line up at the starting line.

HARE: I'm going to leave you behind in my dust.

TORTOISE: No problem. I'm used to dust. I'll just take it slow and steady.

Green Kangaroo Word Search

See if you can find 18 vocabulary words from *The One in the Middle Is the Green Kangaroo* hidden in the puzzle below. Look forward, backward, up, down, and diagonally.

```
S  T  A  G  E  E  I  T  H  E  R  S
T  A  D  M  D  E  P  P  A  L  C  P
O  A  N  I  Q  W  T  P  C  A  F  E
M  A  U  D  I  T  O  R  I  U  M  C
A  C  A  D  W  I  O  B  P  G  M  I
C  N  D  L  R  I  E  W  G  H  I  A
H  R  X  E  U  S  C  R  E  A  M  L
P  I  A  N  C  I  P  H  R  B  P  H
R  P  L  P  R  O  U  D  J  B  O  W
A  E  X  Z  A  H  O  K  N  T  R  C
C  E  C  N  E  I  D  U  A  W  T  M
T  P  L  K  O  O  R  A  G  N  A  K
I  C  O  S  T  U  M  E  Y  E  N  S
C  A  P  L  I  J  G  E  X  A  T  O
E  N  E  I  G  H  B  O  R  S  V  Q
```

━ Word Bank ━

middle	either	kangaroo	practice	costume	laugh
sandwich	special	important	stage	stomach	bow
scream	auditorium	proud	neighbors	audience	clapped

A Star Is Born

Freddy was the star of the show in *The One in the Middle Is the Green Kangaroo*. Have you ever dreamed of being a star? Have you dreamed about being in a movie or television show? Here is your chance to put your dream into words.

If you could be the star of a movie or television show, what would it be? Would you be an action hero, a handsome or beautiful hero of a love story, or a funny star? In the space below, describe what movie or television show you would star in and what you would do as the star.

Quiz

1. On the back of this paper, write a one-paragraph summary of the major events in the first two chapters of *Freckle Juice*.

2. Why does Andrew want freckles? _____

   _____

3. What was Andrew supposed to be doing when he was counting Nicky's freckles? _____

   _____

4. How did Nicky get his freckles? _____

   _____

5. Do you think Andrew likes Sharon? Why or why not? _____

   _____

   _____

6. How much does Andrew have to pay Sharon for the recipe? _____

7. What happened after Andrew bought the recipe from Sharon? _____

   _____

8. Do you think Miss Kelly is a good teacher? Why or why not? _____

   _____

   _____

9. At first, Andrew did not believe Sharon. Why do you think he changed his mind? _____

   _____

   _____

10. Would you buy Sharon's recipe for freckle juice? Why or why not? _____

    _____

    _____

    _____

Fact or Opinion?

Can you tell the difference between a FACT and an OPINION? Mark the following statements as fact or opinion.

?

1. Andrew wants freckles.   FACT   OPINION

2. Freckles are nice.   FACT   OPINION

3. Andrew gets 10 cents allowance each week.   FACT   OPINION

4. Andrew's allowance is not enough.   FACT   OPINION

5. Sharon looks like a frog.   FACT   OPINION

6. Miss Kelly is nice.   FACT   OPINION

7. "Freckle juice" has mustard in it.   FACT   OPINION

8. "Freckle juice" tastes terrible.   FACT   OPINION

9. Andrew's mother plays cards.   FACT   OPINION

10. "Freckle juice" makes Andrew sick.   FACT   OPINION

11. Andrew's dreams are scary.   FACT   OPINION

12. Andrew's "freckles" are blue.   FACT   OPINION

13. The class laughed at Andrew's freckles.   FACT   OPINION

14. Andrew is handsome.   FACT   OPINION

?

I Like Your . . . .

All of us have things about us that are interesting or nice or fun. Andrew likes Nicky's freckles, but other children probably like something about Andrew, too.

In a small group, talk about the things you like about each other. Be sure to find something you like about everyone in your group. Write them below. Use the back of the paper if you need to.

Is there something about the way his or her face and head looks that you like?

- I like _Nicky_ 's _Freckles_ .
- I like _____ 's_____.
- I like _____ 's_____.

Is there something about his or her arms or legs that you like?

- I like _Joe_ 's _long legs_ .
- I like _____ 's_____.
- I like _____ 's_____.

Is there something about the way he or she talks or sings that you like?

- I like the way _Judy_ _sings the marching song_ .
- I like the way _____ _____.
- I like the way _____ _____.

Is there something about the way he or she draws or makes things that you like?

- I like the way _Maria_ _makes leaves from construction paper_ .
- I like the way _____ _____.
- I like the way _____ _____.

Is there something that he or she does that you like?

- I like the way _Angela_ _lends me her scissors_ .
- I like the way _____ _____.
- I like the way _____ _____.

Allowance

You get an allowance of $5.00 per week. On the top half of this page, look at the choices you have to spend your allowance. On the bottom half of this page or on a separate sheet of paper, record how you decide to spend your allowance for the next week. Be sure to add up how much you spend in total and how much is left over.

Friday Night Movie
Movie $2.75
Popcorn $2.00
Drink $1.00

Saturday Skating Party
Skate rental $2.50
Drink $.75
Candy $.75

Watch Videos at Home
Free (Mom buys.)

Going to the Mall
New item for your collection $3.00
Drink $.75

During the Week
Comic book $1.25
Candy $1.75
"Goosebumps" toy $1.50
Bubble gum $.50
New Sega game $17.00

Trip to Washington, D. C.
Your school is planning a field trip to Washington, D. C., in the spring. To go, you must save $1.00 every week from your allowance.

Plan Your Choices Carefully!

Weekend Activity:

Item _____ Cost _____

Item _____ Cost + _____

Item _____ Cost + _____

Item _____ Cost + _____

Total Weekend Cost: _____

During the Week

Item _____ Cost _____

Item _____ Cost + _____

Item _____ Cost + _____

Item _____ Cost + _____

Total During Week Cost: _____

Total Weekend Cost: _____

Total During Week Cost: + _____

Save for Trip: + _____

Total for the Week: _____

How much is left over? _____

Daydreaming

Andrew got caught daydreaming about freckles when he was supposed to be in his reading group. A daydream is like a regular dream except that you are not asleep when you have it. You're awake, but your mind is somewhere else. Do you ever daydream at home or at school? What do you daydream about? In the space below, describe a daydream you have had. Close your eyes for a minute if it helps you think.

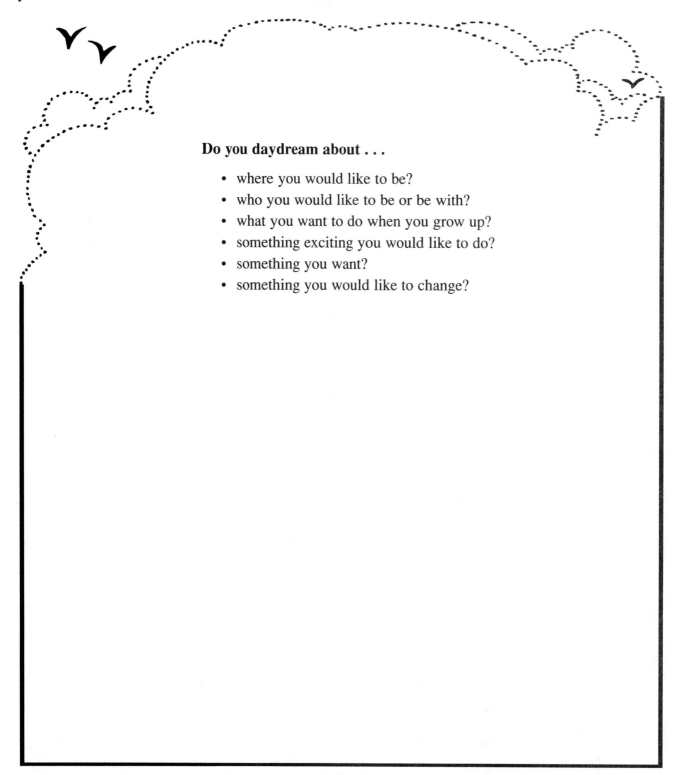

Do you daydream about . . .

- where you would like to be?
- who you would like to be or be with?
- what you want to do when you grow up?
- something exciting you would like to do?
- something you want?
- something you would like to change?

Quiz

1. On the back of this paper, write a one-paragraph summary of the major events in the last three chapters of *Freckle Juice*.

2. Why wasn't Andrew's mother home when he came home from school? _____

   _____

3. Name at least three ingredients in the secret recipe for freckle juice. _____

   _____

4. Would you ever eat or drink something as disgusting as freckle juice if doing so could get you something? Why or why not? _____

   _____

   _____

5. Why was Andrew's mother scared when she came home? _____

   _____

6. Why didn't Andrew want to go to school after he was well? _____

   _____

7. Why does the class laugh at Andrew's freckles? _____

   _____

8. How much does Miss Kelly's secret formula cost Andrew? _____

   _____

9. What does Andrew do with Miss Kelly's secret formula? _____

   _____

10. Do you think Nicky will buy Sharon's secret formula for freckle remover? Why or why not?

    _____

    _____

    _____

No-Cook Recipe Fun

Sharon's recipe for freckle juice did not need cooking. There are many good things you can make without cooking. Follow the recipe your teacher assigns to your group and then have a class picnic!

Pudding

Ingredients:
1 box of pudding mix
2 cups (500 mL) of milk
1 large mixing bowl
1 whisk or eggbeater
bowls for serving

Directions:
1. Pour milk into mixing bowl.
2. Open pudding mix and pour on top of milk.
3. Beat or whisk for two minutes.
4. Pour into serving bowls.

Peanut Butter Quarters

Ingredients:
1 jar of peanut butter
1 jar of jelly
1 loaf of bread
1 knife
plate for serving

Directions:
1. Open peanut butter and jelly.
2. Get two slices of bread from loaf.
3. Spread peanut butter on one slice of bread.
4. Spread jelly on the other slice of bread.
5. Put slices together into a sandwich.
6. Cut the sandwich into quarters for serving.

Chocolate Milk

Ingredients:
1 gallon (3.8 L) of milk
1 can of chocolate milk mix
1 large measuring cup
1 spoon
cups for the class

Directions:
1. Fill the measuring cup with milk.
2. Look to see how many cups of milk are in the measuring cup.
3. Add one spoonful of mix for every cup of milk.
4. Stir until well mixed.
5. Pour into cups for serving.

Applewiches

Ingredients:
1 bowl of apple slices
1 bowl of cheese slices
1 box of toothpicks
plate for serving

Directions:
1. Take two slices of apple out of the bowl.
2. Take one slice of cheese out of the bowl.
3. Make a sandwich by putting the cheese between the apple slices.
4. Put a toothpick through the sandwich.
5. Put the sandwich on a plate for serving.

Bumps on a Log

Ingredients:
1 bowl of celery sticks
1 jar of peanut butter
1 box of raisins
1 knife
plate for serving

Directions:
1. Take one stick of celery from the bowl.
2. Spread peanut butter on the celery.
3. Put raisins on top of the peanut butter.
4. Put on a plate for serving.

34

Make a Recipe

A recipe gives the instructions for making something. It includes a list of all the ingredients needed and also the directions for mixing them together.

In your group, choose something you want to write a recipe for. Decide what ingredients go into the recipe and then estimate how much of each ingredient is needed. Finally, write directions for mixing them together, cooking them, or anything else you think needs to be done.

Our Recipe for _____

Ingredients	How Much?
_____	_____
_____	_____
_____	_____
_____	_____
_____	_____
_____	_____
_____	_____
_____	_____

Directions

1. _____
   _____

2. _____
   _____

3. _____
   _____

4. _____
   _____

5. _____
   _____

Chemistry Experiments

Chemistry experiments are a lot like recipes. You need to gather ingredients, measure them carefully, follow directions exactly, and be very careful while you do the experiment. Here are some chemistry experiments you can do with a partner. Your teacher will show you where to get the ingredients and tools you need.

> **Be Safe:** Chemicals can be very dangerous. Never touch, smell, or taste any chemical unless your teacher or parent says it is safe. Mixing two materials together can make a dangerous reaction. Some will catch on fire. Others will explode. Some will burn your skin or make dangerous gas. Always do chemistry experiments with adult supervision!

Make It Pop

Materials:
$1/2$ cup (125 mL) vinegar
$1 1/2$ teaspoons (7.5 mL) baking soda
1 bottle
1 cork
1 piece of tissue paper

Procedure:
1. Pour the vinegar into the bottle.
2. Lay the tissue paper flat and pour the baking soda on it.
3. Gather the corners of the paper and twist them together to hold the baking soda.
4. Drop the tissue paper bundle into the bottle.
5. Quickly put the cork in the bottle but not too tightly.
6. Shake the bottle once or twice.
7. Stand away from the bottle and see what happens.

Results:
Combining the vinegar and baking soda makes a gas, carbon dioxide, which expands inside the bottle. The cork is then forced to pop out of the bottle.

Rising Yeast

Materials:

1 package dry yeast
1 tablespoon sugar
2 empty cups
1 cup warm water

Procedure:
1. Pour half the package of yeast into one cup and half into the other cup.
2. Pour the sugar into one of the cups. Put an X on that cup.
3. Pour half the water into one cup and half into the other cup.
4. Watch what happens in the two cups. What do you smell?

Results:
Yeast is a plant that uses sugar as a food. It breaks down the sugar into carbon dioxide and alcohol. Carbon dioxide is a gas that makes bubbles in the water. When we make bread, the bubbles make the bread rise. The smell is the same that you smell when bread is baking.

I Like My . . .

In the end, Andrew was happy with himself, even without freckles. Think about yourself for a minute. What are all the things you like about yourself? Write your thoughts in the space below. Use these questions to help you think.

- What do I like about the way I look?
- What do I like about the way I act?
- What do I like about the way I feel?
- What makes me who I am?

Book Report Ideas

There are many ways to report on a book once you have read it. After you have finished reading the three books, choose one method of reporting on them that interests you. It may be an idea of your own or one of the ways mentioned below.

Show Me

Construct a model of a scene from one of the books, using a shoebox as a diorama or drawing the scene on paper.

In My Opinion

Choose two of the books and tell which one you liked better. Explain why you formed this opinion by comparing the two books and giving examples from the stories.

The Sequel

You have probably seen movie sequels or read sequels to books you enjoyed. Write "part two" of one of the three books, predicting what might happen to the characters if the story were continued.

If You Liked This One . . .

Select two of the books. Pretend that your audience has read one of the books and it is now your job to persuade them to read the second book. You might start your report by saying, "If you liked (name of the book), you will really like . . . ." Persuade your audience by reminding them of funny or dramatic scenes or characters in the first book and telling them about similar things in the second book.

Talk Show Interview

This can be done by any size group. One student will pretend to be a talk show host. Every other student will pretend to be a character from one of the books. The host will read questions prepared by the "characters." Each "character" will answer the questions, trying to provide the audience with insights into the character's personality and life.

Twenty Clues

Choose a character, event, or object from one of the books. Give clues to the class and have them try to guess who or what you have chosen. Begin with very general clues and then get more specific. If the class does not guess after 20 clues, tell them the answer.

Don't Miss It

Pretend that one of the books has been made into a television special. Design a magazine or newspaper advertisement for the show. Include the name of the book and the author, the actors who will be in the show, a picture of a character or scene from the show, and a brief description of the story that will make people want to watch.

Crossword Puzzle

Get out your vocabulary lists for the three books. Some of the words are in this puzzle.

Across

1. musical instrument with keys
3. Pay _____ in school!
6. where sick people stay
8. food: oval, green, small
9. after dinner treat
10. car with a siren
13. clothes for a play
14. nice-looking
16. why you do something
20. normal
21. not first or last
23. bend at the waist
24. part of your mouth
25. ha, ha, ha!
26. something that matters a lot
27. think about something that happened

Down

1. what you should be when you do well
2. next-door _____
3. weekly money
4. recipe parts
5. do over and over to get better
7. yucky
11. this one or that one
12. Australian animal
15. part of a gallon
17. watch plays here
18. growls when you're hungry
19. what your brain makes
22. "I don't want any more. I've had _____."

A Play About Families

Plan Your Scene

In *The Pain and the Great One*, *The One in the Middle Is the Green Kangaroo*, and *Freckle Juice*, we read about three different kinds of families. The first had two children, the second had three, and the third had one.

Your class is going to create a play about families. Your teacher will assign you to groups to write and perform one scene in the play. First, you must choose a family to write about. Get out your paper from "My Family" (page 22). Read it to your group. As a group, choose something from one of the papers to write your scene about. It should be something that will be easy to act out for your classmates. It should not embarrass anyone or hurt anyone's feelings. Make sure everyone in the group agrees that your choice is a good one. When you finish, get your teacher's approval for your idea.

Now, brainstorm ideas for your scene. Assign someone to be the scribe who will write down the ideas as they come up. The scribe should write down every idea, no matter how crazy it might sound. If your group runs out of ideas, have the scribe read the ideas that you've already had. They may give someone another idea. The only rule for brainstorming is this: everyone has ideas, and no one can make fun of them! Here are some questions to get your ideas started.

- What characters could be in the scene?
- Where could the scene take place?
- Would the scene be funny or serious?
- Will you need a narrator to explain what is happening, or will the lines the characters speak explain it?
- Will you need any costumes for the characters, or will your normal clothes work?
- How can you start the scene? How can you end it?
- How long do you think the scene will take? (Your teacher may give you help with this.)
- What will the title of the scene be?

When you run out of ideas, or when your teacher says to stop, have the scribe read all the ideas to the group. Everyone else should listen quietly. Then have the scribe read each idea, one at a time, and have the group decide whether it should stay on the list or not. Now is the time to start deciding exactly what your scene will be like. After you get to the end of the list, you may want to have someone in the group copy it so it is easier to read.

Now you are ready to go on to the second part of the activity—writing your scene!

A Play About Families *(cont.)*

Write and Rehearse Your Scene

Get out your group's list of ideas. Use your list to fill out the following sheet for your scene about a family. It is all right to change it as you go along. You may think of ideas that work better after you write part of the scene.

- ### Characters

    Write the names of the characters in your group's scene and a brief description of who they are. Your scene should have no more characters than the number in your group.

    Example: Name: <u>Jamie</u>   Description: <u>third grade boy</u>

- ### Setting

    Tell where and when the scene happens.

    Example: Where: <u>at the dining room table</u>   When: <u>Sunday afternoon</u>

- ### Lines

    Get out your paper with the scene of the play about the Tortoise and the Hare (page 25). Study how the lines the characters say are written. You should write your lines the same way. First, write the name of the character who will say the line. Then write the line the character will say. If there are any actions a character needs to make, write those between the lines and within parentheses.

    Example:

    MOM: Eat your peas, Jamie.

    (Jamie holds his stomach and makes a face.)

    JAMIE: But Mom, peas make me sick to my stomach!

Assign someone to be the scribe for your group again. The scribe should not be the same person as last time. As a group, decide what the first line for your scene should be. Then have the scribe write the line. (If your class has a computer and your teacher approves, you might want to write the lines on the computer.) Write the second line by deciding what to say and then having the scribe write it. Keep making up lines until the scene is done. Then have the scribe read it back to the group. Make any changes the group agrees to. When you are finished, have your teacher check it and make suggestions. (If your scene is very long, your teacher might want to check it halfway through.)

When you and your teacher are happy with your scene, it is time to assign the characters to your group members. If there are fewer characters than group members, try to decide who will be in the scene and who will not. If your group cannot decide, talk to your teacher.

To rehearse the scene, follow the instructions from your tortoise-and-hare scene.

Your teacher will decide what order the scenes will be performed in. Be polite and pay attention when the other groups perform their scenes. When it is your group's turn, stand up straight and speak loudly. Break a leg!

A Play About Families *(cont.)*

Group _____

Scene _____

Characters

Name:_____ Description: _____
Name:_____ Description: _____
Name:_____ Description: _____
Name:_____ Description: _____

Setting

Where: _____

When: _____

Lines

_____: _____
_____

_____: _____
_____

_____: _____
_____

_____: _____
_____

_____: _____
_____

_____: _____
_____

_____: _____
_____

_____: _____

Use a separate sheet of paper for more lines.

Unit Test

Matching: Match the quote with the person who said it. Write the speakers' names in the correct blanks.

- The Pain
- The Great One
- Freddy Dissel
- Andrew
- Sharon
- Miss Kelly

1. "Here's your note, Andrew. I have a feeling it's important to you. But from now on you must pay attention in class!"_____

2. "She thinks she's great just because she can play the piano and you can tell the songs are real ones."_____

3. "It'll cost you fifty cents. I have a secret recipe for freckle juice."_____

4. "He's not supposed to get dessert unless he eats his meat. But he always gets it anyway."_____

5. "I grew freckles, Miss Kelly. That's what!"_____

6. "He felt like the peanut butter in a sandwich, squeezed between Mike and Ellen."_____

True or False: Write true or false next to each statement.

7. _____ The Great One is older than The Pain.

8. _____ Freddy is the oldest child.

9. _____ The audience liked Freddy in the play.

10. _____ Freckle juice works!

11. _____ Andrew liked the taste of freckle juice.

Short Answer: On a separate piece of paper, provide a short answer for each of these questions. Be sure to clearly number each of your answers.

12. Why does The Great One get mad at The Pain when she is playing blocks with her friends?

13. What grade is Freddy in?

14. What did Ms. Matson do at the end of the play to give Freddy special attention?

15. Describe how Andrew pays for and gets the recipe for freckle juice from Sharon.

16. What did Andrew do on the way to school after he drank freckle juice?

Essay: Answer these questions on a separate piece of paper.

17. Give examples of how your family is like or not like the families in *The Pain and the Great One* and *The One in the Middle Is the Green Kangaroo.* Give at least five examples.

18. Describe the steps Andrew went through to make freckle juice.

Response

Directions: Explain the meaning of each of these quotes from *The Pain and the Great One, The One in the Middle Is the Green Kangaroo,* and *Freckle Juice.*

The Pain and the Great One

- *She says ooh and aah over all his pictures, which aren't great at all, but just ordinary first grade stuff.*
- *I think they love him better than me.*
- *When she dials she never gets the wrong person.*

The One in the Middle Is the Green Kangaroo

- *He felt like the peanut butter part of a sandwich.*
- *His heart started to beat faster. His stomach bounced up and down. He felt funny.*
- *He didn't even care much about being the one in the middle.*

Freckle Juice

- *Sharon's tongue reminded Andrew of a frog catching flies.*
- *"Sorry, Andrew. A deal's a deal!" Sharon opened a book and pretended to read.*
- *"After tomorrow I won't have any trouble paying attention," he promised. "Just you wait, Miss Kelly. I won't have any trouble at all."*
- *That old Sharon! She probably thought he wouldn't be able to drink it. Well, he'd show her.*
- *"Oh my! Appendicitis! You must have appendicitis! I'm going to call the doctor. No, I'd better just drive straight to the hospital. No, I'll call the ambulance!"*
- *Maybe they didn't look like Nicky Lane's freckles, but they looked like something!*

Teacher Note: Choose an appropriate number of quotes for your students.

Conversations

Work in groups to write and perform the conversations that might have occurred in each of the following situations.

The Pain and the Great One

◆ The Pain and The Great One are having dinner. (2 people)
◆ The Great One and The Pain go swimming. (2 people)
◆ The Great One's friends build a city from blocks, and The Pain wrecks it. (several people)

The One in the Middle Is the Green Kangaroo

◆ Freddy tries out for the play for Ms. Matson. (2 people)
◆ Freddy tells his family he will be in the play. (several people)
◆ Freddy gets ready for the play backstage. (several people)

Freckle Juice

◆ Andrew gets caught daydreaming instead of going to reading group. (several people)
◆ Sharon offers to sell Andrew the secret recipe for freckle juice. (2 people)
◆ Andrew gets the secret recipe from Miss Kelly at the end of the day. (2 people)
◆ Andrew gets the key from his mother. (2 people)
◆ Andrew's mother finds him after he drinks the freckle juice. (2 people)
◆ Miss Kelly tells Andrew he is handsome without freckles and tells Nicky he is handsome with freckles. (3 people)

Think of your own conversation idea for the characters in one of the books. Write your conversation idea on the lines below.

_____

_____

_____

_____

_____

Bibliography

Related Reading

Blume, Judy. *Superfudge*. Dutton, 1980.

Castiglia, Julie. *Jill the Pill*. Atheneum, 1979.

Cleary, Beverly. *Ramona Quimby, Age Eight*. Morrow, 1981.

Fox, Paula. *The Stone-Faced Boy*. Bradbury, 1968.

Hoban, Lillian. *Arthur's Pen Pal*. Harper LB, 1976.

Labin, Patricia. *Oh, Brother!* Little, 1987.

Udry, Janice May. *How I Faded Away*. Albert Whitman, 1976.

Baseball Movies

Bad News Bears. (Videotape) Paramount Picture Corporation. Paramount Home Video, 1988.

The 50 Greatest Home Runs in Baseball History. (Videotape) Major League Baseball Productions. Major League Baseball Home Video, 1992.

A League of Their Own. (Videotape) Columbia Pictures. Columbia TriStar Home Video, 1992.

The Natural. (Videotape) TriStar Pictures. RCA/Columbia Pictures Home Video, 1984.

Chemistry Experiments

Challand, Helen J. *Experiments with Chemistry*. Children's Press, 1988.

Cobb, Vicki. *Science Experiments You Can Eat*. Scholastic Inc., 1972.

Dramatic Production

Coody, Betty. *Using Literature with Young Children, 4th Edition*. William C. Brown Publishers, 1992.

Judy, Susan and Stephen Judy. *Putting on a Play: A Guide to Writing and Producing Neighborhood Drama*. Charles Scribner's Sons, 1982.

Ross, Beverly and Jean Durgin. *Junior Broadway*. McFarland, 1983.

Answer Key

Page 12

1. Accept appropriate responses.
2. A little brother
3. A big sister
4. Accept 3 appropriate answers.
5. Accept 3 appropriate answers.
6. The Great One
7. There is nothing to do.
8. Accept appropriate responses.
9. Accept appropriate responses.
10. Accept appropriate responses.

Page 13

1. Cat
2. Pain
3. Mom
4. Pain
5. Great One
6. Mom or Dad
7. Great One
8. Mom
9. Pain
10. Pain
11. Great One

Page 17

1. Accept appropriate responses.
2. older, younger
3. Accept appropriate responses.
4. to the auditorium
5. yell and jump
6. 5th and 6th
7. choked and spilled his milk
8. Accept appropriate responses.
9. Accept appropriate responses.
10. Accept appropriate responses.

Page 23

1. Accept appropriate responses.
2. jumped and practiced his lines
3. his class, his family, his neighbors
4. good luck

5. Accept appropriate responses.
6. He was nervous.
7. Accept appropriate responses.
8. jump around the stage and say he was the Green Kangaroo
9. Yes. They laughed and clapped.
10. Accept appropriate responses.

Page 26

Page 28

1. Accept appropriate responses.
2. so he doesn't have to wash his neck
3. going to reading group
4. He was born with them.
5. Accept appropriate responses.
6. fifty cents
7. Miss Kelly caught them and took away the recipe.
8. Accept appropriate responses.
9. Accept appropriate responses.
10. Accept appropriate responses.

Answer Key *(cont.)*

Page 29

1. Fact
2. Opinion
3. Fact
4. Opinion
5. Opinion
6. Opinion
7. Fact
8. Opinion
9. Fact
10. Fact
11. Opinion
12. Fact
13. Fact
14. Opinion

Page 33

1. Accept appropriate responses.
2. She was at the neighbor's house.
3. Accept appropriate responses.
4. Accept appropriate responses.
5. Andrew was sick and lying on the floor.
6. He didn't want Sharon to see him without freckles.
7. They are blue.
8. nothing
9. He uses it to wash off his Magic Marker freckles.
10. Accept appropriate responses.

Page 39

Page 43

1. Miss Kelly
2. The Pain
3. Sharon
4. The Great One
5. Andrew
6. Freddy
7. True
8. False
9. True
10. False
11. False
12. He knocks down the blocks.
13. 2nd grade
14. She let him bow by himself.
15. He threw the money on the floor. Sharon picked it up and threw the recipe back. Miss Kelly caught them.
16. He drew freckles on his face with blue Magic Marker.
17. Accept appropriate responses.
18. Accept appropriate responses.